I0429349

INCREASE PRODUCTIVITY

5 QUICK HACKS: A GUIDE TO IDEAS THAT WILL
FREE UP YOUR TIME AND END
PROCRASTINATION

Need a quick productivity boost?

Everybody has the same amount of time in a day – 24 hours – yet some people seem to get a lot more done than others.

In this book we are going to look at 5 quick and easy ways to increase our productivity today, using the methods practiced by those who seem to get everything done!

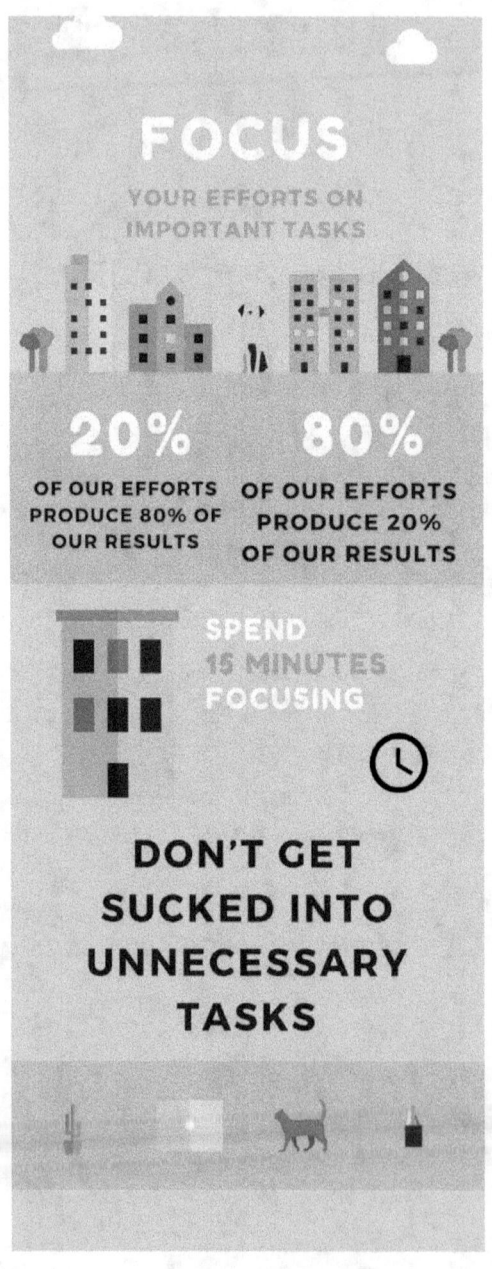

Lack of focus on the right tasks not only makes your day less productive but this bad habit can affect your personal and work life. Pareto's law states that 80% of the outputs result from 20% of the inputs. This means that 20% of our actions result in 80% of the results. It is important to spend your 'focus' time on that 20% that is creating the 80% of our desired outcomes, and spend our time on that alone.

Don't get sucked into unnecessary tasks because they seem to result in instant gratification. Sometimes we feel that if there is not an instant reward, it is not worth doing. This is far from the truth. Ask yourself, 'Am I only doing this to get an immediate reward, or is it also going to help me achieve my goals?'.

Focus on this for 15 minutes at a time.

Take 15 minute chunks of time to do something pressing. You may even surprise yourself and finish a task completely. Put headphones on with a 15 minute playlist of songs or an audiobook, and focus only on ONE task. Do not stop until the 15 minutes is up. I tell my children that if my headphones are in, for that 15 minutes they cannot interrupt me, unless it's urgent, for instance a broken arm or an earthquake.

It doesn't matter if you hate the task. Just think – it's only 15 minutes, and when this 15 minutes is over, I'll never have to repeat those 15 minutes again. I will feel better in myself, because I will no longer have to dread this task, because it will be completed!

1. Remove distractions

REMOVE DISTRACTIONS

Distractions include email, the phone, TV and the internet.

Social media is a big player when it comes to distraction. Stay focused, turn your phone on silent, resist the urge to see what your cousins best friends boyfriend has just caught on his fishing trip – you can catch up when your tasks are completed, and you will be more relaxed when doing so.

Set limits for yourself for unproductive internet or TV usage. Maybe you have a favourite show that you like to watch every week – make sure you factor this in. Productivity is great, but you still need to have 'down' time.

2. Get Some Sleep

Sleep can become a long lost memory when we are trying to achieve so many things at once, and may even seem like a waste of 'productive' hours. It is important to get plenty of sleep, at least 6-8 hours per night, so that your waking hours can be as productive as possible.

Sleep can also prevent that 'brain fog' that many of us experience, and leads to a lack of motivation. If you are one of those people that cuts out sleep to get more done, you will probably find Joe Bloggs who gets his 7.5 hours sleep every night achieves a lot more than you do.

Set a bed time each day, and try not to stimulate yourself too much the hour beforehand. This can perhaps be your time to catch up on your favourite TV show, social media, or that book that has been sitting on your bedside table for three months – just make sure it is not about productivity – as this could start your mind racing.

3. Lists

Yes, we think we are being productive when making our lists, but much of the time we are slowing the process down. As procrastinators, we generally do love our lists, but they could be a cause of the problem.

Invariably, our lists are too long to be achievable, or there are many lists. I know I have about five on the go at any one time, perhaps to remind me of what I need to do when I finally decide to do them. This long list makes you feel overwhelmed, and you are more likely to – you guessed it – procrastinate. You can still make lists, but, there is a better, more effective way to do them.

Take 30 seconds – only 30 seconds, and no longer – to list down the tasks you feel are most urgent at the moment. Commit to not writing any more lists until this list is completed. Hopefully you only come up with two or three tasks, if you have more, prioritise and pick the top three ONLY. If you put too much on there, you are likely to procrastinate, and achieve nothing.

4. Employ daily routines

MY WORK DAY

Start Work
9:00

Morning Tea
10:30-10.45

Lunch Break
12:30-1:30

Afternoon Tea
3:00-3:15

Finish Work
5:00

Robert Collier once said, "Success they say is the sum of small efforts, repeated day in and day out."

I like to have morning and evening routines, but do what is best for you. When you hop out of bed in the morning, it takes less than a minute to make your bed, so do this first.

Use your time in the shower to go over the things in your head that you would like to achieve today, or that NEED to be achieved – that requirement at work, or the toilet paper that needs to be restocked. While brushing your teeth, think about HOW you intend to achieve these. Break things down, don't overwhelm yourself. After this, write down a 30 second list, as suggested above.

Conclusion

So there you have it! Start implementing any of the above five steps into your daily life, and you should start seeing results very soon. Enjoy being productive!

Free Content: 21 Off The Wall Business Ideas

21 off the wall business ideas to start in 2016

Collaborated from highly talented research projects sponsored by the likes of Forbes, Money Magazine, **Fortune**.com and Business Review Weekly. We have compiled a list of the most lucrative and "outside the box" business ideas based on consumer trends for the year 2016.

The list covers a range of sectors, beauty, health, social media, business, and construction amongst others, so wherever your interests lay there is sure be something that is workable for you.

1. App Development

While mainly dominated by games, consumers are moving towards using apps that help streamline their day to day life – from shopping lists, to checking out reviews for a restaurant they are interested in. Most consumers with a mobile phone have a smart phone, and for ease of use are downloading apps. There are plenty of apps that are not yet created, so there is plenty of room to make a successful business out of this.

WORLDWIDE MOBILE APP DOWNLOADS

 2015

 2014

 2013

 2012

179,628,000

NUMBER OF MOBILE
APP DOWLOADS IN
2015

138,809,000

NUMBER OF MOBILE
APP DOWLOADS IN
2014

102,062,000

NUMBER OF MOBILE
APP DOWLOADS IN
2013

63,985,000

NUMBER OF MOBILE
APP DOWLOADS IN
2012

2. Video Production and Animation

Every month Youtube has over one billion views, with an average of six billion hours spent watching videos. Some forecast that 55% of consumer internet traffic will be made up of online video. Businesses are becoming increasingly aware of the need to market in this genre, and will be looking for skilled technicians to work it out for them.

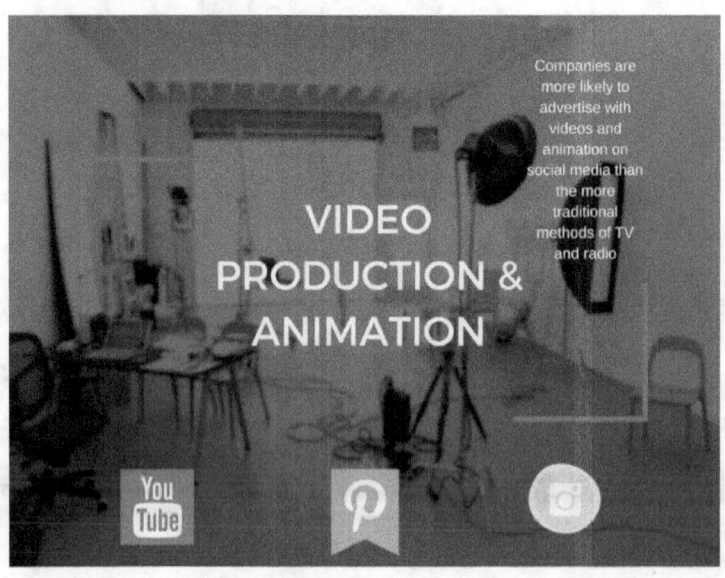

3. Online Speed Dating Service

This is a mixture of Speed Dating and Online Dating. Both are growing sectors, although online dating is growing faster. Why not mix the two? This can be an easy business to set up, customers prepay, and you can book a restaurant or event location with set price meals or drinks. You can have a lot of fun with this one!

SPEED DATING!
FINDING TRUE LOVE

FACTS

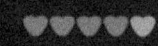

- MOST COMMON AGES ARE BETWEEN 16-34
- SINGLE WOMEN OUTNUMBER MEN BY 230,000 IN NEW YORK CITY

70%

MEN WHO RECEIVE POSITIVE MATCHES

♥♥♥♥♥

4 IN 5 WOMEN REPORT A POSITIVE SPEED DATING EXPERIENCE

50 percent of all relationships could begin online by 2031. By 2040, that number could jump to 70 percent

SOURCES: HTTP://WWW.NYEASYDATES.COM EHARMONY LAUNCHES A NEW SITE FOR SPANISH-SPEAKING SINGLES

4. Designated Driver Service

This involves being available for those who want to go out, have a drink or two, and want a reliable lift to get them home, or to their next destination. Obviously, you will need to set some groundrules with potential clients, and make these clear from the start.

5. Gigwalking

Gigwalk is a free smartphone app where you can sign up and locals get you to complete small or large tasks for them. You can specialise in any field you fancy, or pick a few!

6. Human Billboard

No, this doesn't mean you need to tattoo a company's name on your forehead! This could include holding or wearing a sign with a business's advertisement, and if you are the shy type, it can still be profitable by hiring subcontractors.

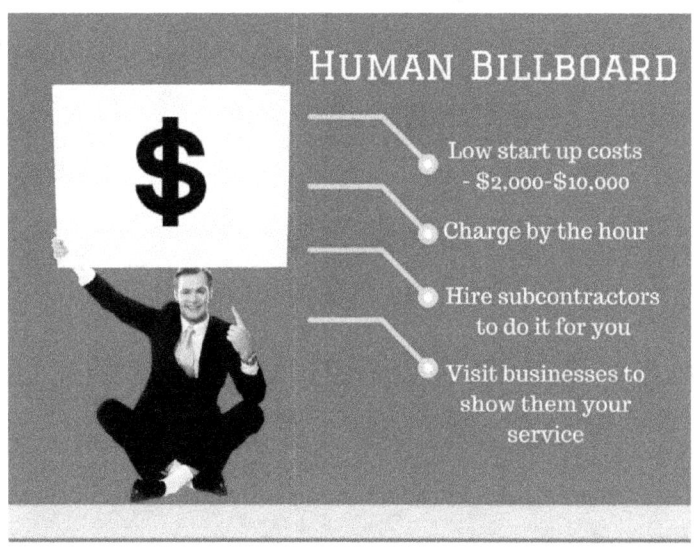

7. Renting out your car

Apparently the average car is sitting unused for 22 hours a day, so why not look at hiring it out for some of those. You could drive to the office, and hire your car from there, ensuring it is returned by the time you need to head

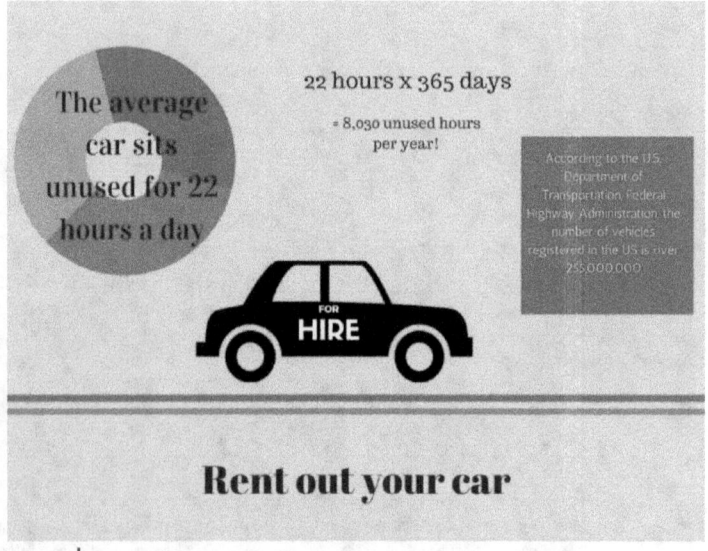

home!

8. Teaching on Udemy

There are tons of consumers who are now looking for education online, rather than going to a physical school. Udemy offers lots of help setting these up, so if you have knowledge in a particular area, share it with the world.

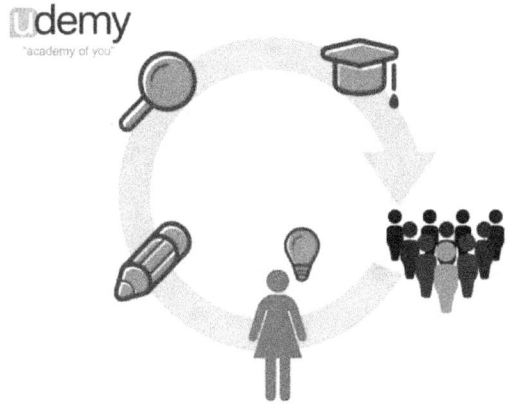

9. Tour Guide

Just as the title suggests, you could offer tour guides around your local area to travellers. These could be driven tours, or walking tours. A great opportunity if you are a people person.

TOUR GUIDE
THE NEXT BIG THING

SEE THE WORLD WHILE SHOWING OTHERS

GET TO KNOW

YOUR AREA

EARN $

10. Bicycle Taxi

4 SIMPLE STEPS FOR

BICYCLE TAXI

Every year thousands of people are injured and hundreds of people are killed while riding bicycles.

① PROTECT YOUR HEAD

Always wear a helmet.

② OBEY ALL TRAFFIC LAWS & LIGHTS

Bicycles must follow the rules of the road like other vehicles.

③ ACT LIKE A CAR

Drivers are used to the patterns of other drivers. Don't weave in and out of traffic. The more predictably you ride, the safer you are. Check for traffic. Be aware of traffic around you.

④ USE HAND SIGNALS

Hand signals tell motorists and pedestrians what you intend to do. Signal as a matter of law, of courtesy, and of self-protection.

YOU ARE GOOD TO GO!

Stay safe

An example of this is running in Amsterdam at the moment called Yellow Backie, allowing hitchhikers to be picked up on a bicycle and enjoy the sights at an easier pace while on their way to their next destination.

11. 3D Printing

3D printing will be so important in the coming years, and has already made life changing results, for example artificial limbs. 3D printers are becoming increasingly affordable as their popularity rises.

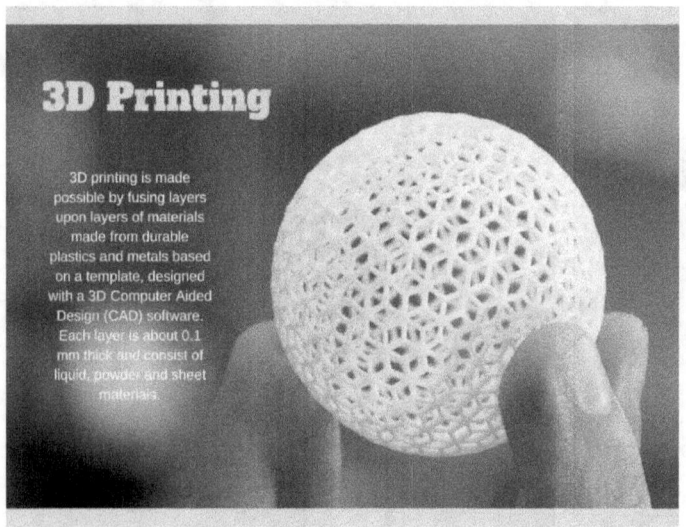

12. Instagram Consulting

Many businesses are heading to Instagram for marketing, but do not yet know how to use this properly. If you are an Instagram junkie, you probably already have a good working knowledge.

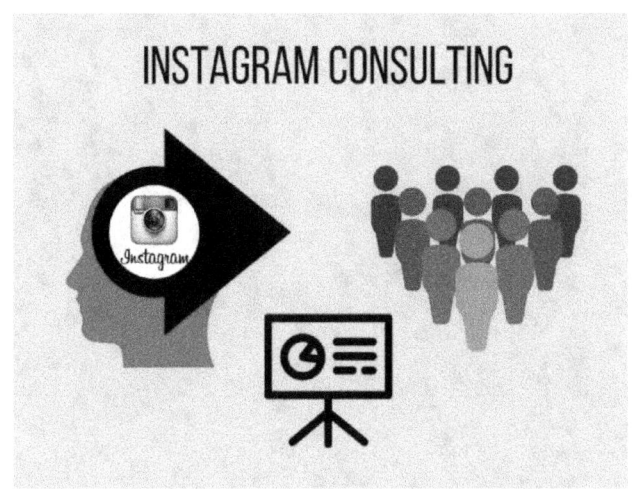

13. Small House Building

As owning a house becomes less and less attainable for some – either through pricing, or finding space – small houses are becoming very popular, due to the reduced cost compared to an average house, and the shorter time periods it takes to build them.

14. 24 hour gyms

With our busy lives today, gyms are not always easily accessible. 24 hour gyms have really taken off, and involves giving paid members a key to the gym, to be able to use whenever they want, even if it is 4am in the morning.

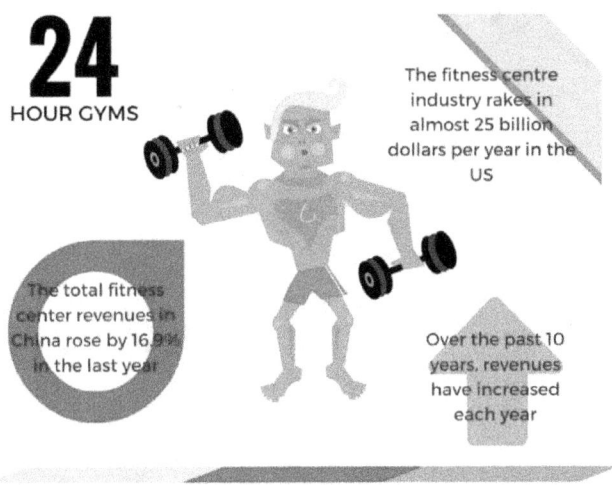

24
HOUR GYMS

The fitness centre industry rakes in almost 25 billion dollars per year in the US

The total fitness center revenues in China rose by 16.9% in the last year

Over the past 10 years, revenues have increased each year

15. Restaurant review websites

Rather than taking the risk of a bad night out, and food poisoning, consumers are now looking for reviews for their local restaurants before booking a table. Consider setting up a site that the everyday connoisseur can leave reviews on.

Restaurant

Review

Websites

16. Social good consultant

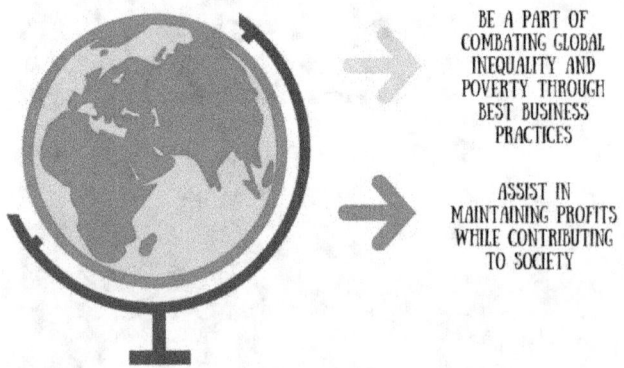

Social Good Consultant

BE A PART OF COMBATING GLOBAL INEQUALITY AND POVERTY THROUGH BEST BUSINESS PRACTICES

ASSIST IN MAINTAINING PROFITS WHILE CONTRIBUTING TO SOCIETY

It is becoming the norm for businesses to adopt 'social good' practices, and many need help with how to set this up. Social good covers many aspects, from fair trade, to offering employment to the underprivileged.

17. Halal Beauty

Halal beauty is a fast growing trend, that is said to be worth billions of dollars. While many beauty products contain pig fat, for example lipsticks, Halal products only contain Halal certified ingredients. The stats speak for themselves, and these products are not only purchased for religious reasons, but

3 out of 10
BeauTY ProDUCTS SOLD In MaLaYSia are HaLaL

Source: The International Trade and Industry Deputy Minister of Malaysia, Datuk Mukhriz Mahathir

for their 'healthier' aspect also.

18. Beauty Foods

They say you are what you eat, and consumers are becoming increasingly aware of this, but do need some guidance. Beauty foods are not only eaten, but are also used in beauty products for their antiaging and beautifying properties.

19. Natural Beauty

Organic and natural beauty products are only increasing in popularity, as consumers are made more aware of the toxins in the environment, and those that they are applying to their body. Ingredients are one of the first things to be looked at by beauty consumers.

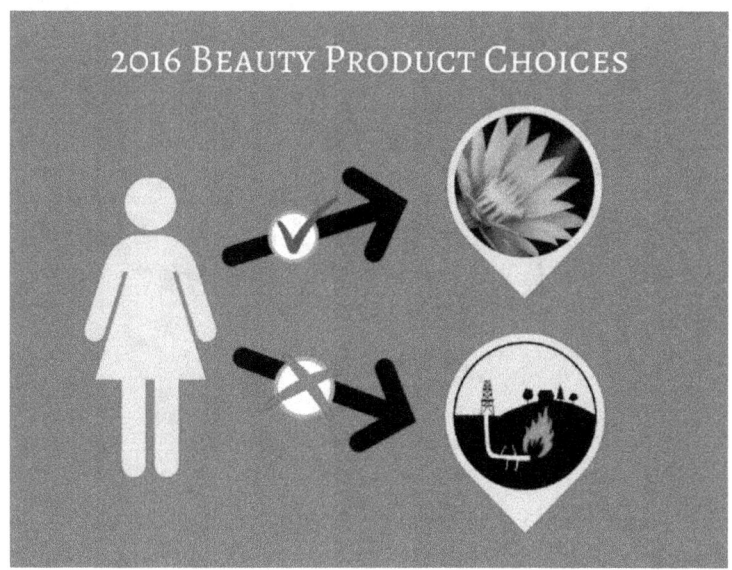

20. Co-Working spaces

As more and more people work from home, the need to still be around others and to find a workable working space is integral. Many local governments have seen this need, and are providing these spaces.

A recent survey by Deskmag found:

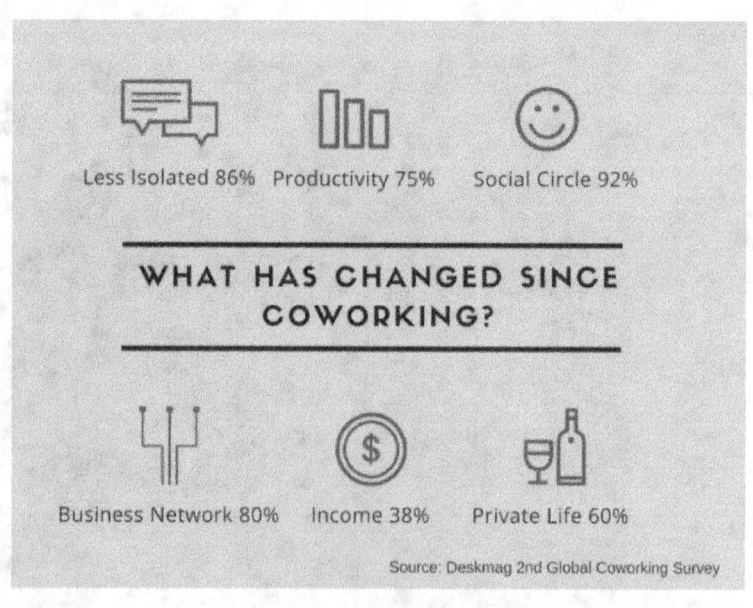

Less Isolated 86% Productivity 75% Social Circle 92%

WHAT HAS CHANGED SINCE COWORKING?

Business Network 80% Income 38% Private Life 60%

Source: Deskmag 2nd Global Coworking Survey

21. Web Traffic Consultant

Whereas business before would hire a marketing guru to come into their business, make banners, logos, etc – the are now heading online. Marketing is free through facebook, twitter, Instagram, so easily accessible for them. What they don't know how to do though, is market correctly, recognise trends, or find their target market to get more web traffic, if any at all

Website
Traffic
Consultant

71%

Businesses planning to increase their digital marketing budgets (Source: Webbiquity)

1/3

Businesses are planning to introduce a Digital Transformation programme (Source: Smart Insights and TFM&A)

3 X

Content marketing in 2015 produces 3 times as many leads as standard outbound marketing, but costs 62% less. (Source: HubSpot)